What Are the Promises I Make at
BAPTISM?

Written by *Michele Leigh Carnesecca*

Illustrated by *Carol Shelley Xanthos*

DESERET
BOOK

Salt Lake City, Utah

Text © 2011 Michele Leigh Carnesecca

Illustrations © 2011 Carol Shelley Xanthos

Visit us at DeseretBook.com

Library of Congress Cataloging-in-Publication Data
Carnesecca, Michele Leigh, author.
  What are the promises I make at baptism? / Michele Leigh Carnesecca ; illustrated by Carol Shelley Xanthos.
     pages   cm.
  Summary: A book for children about the covenants they make when they are baptized.
  ISBN 978-1-60641-953-3 (hardbound : alk. paper)
  1. Latter-day Saint children—Religious life—Juvenile literature.   2. Baptism—Juvenile literature.   I. Xanthos, Carol Shelley, illustrator.   II. Title.
    BX8655.3.C37 2011
    234'.161—dc22   2010044125

Printed in New Jersey, USA by Lehigh Phoenix   5/2011
10 9 8 7 6 5 4 3 2 1

Introduction

Our Heavenly Father loves us and wants us to be happy and return to live with Him. But two things stop us from returning to Him:

1. We all sin (Romans 3:23).
2. We all die (2 Nephi 9:6).

Because our Heavenly Father loves us, He sent His perfect Son, Jesus Christ, to help us overcome sin and death. Jesus paid for our sins in the Garden of Gethsemane and on the cross at Calvary so that we can be forgiven. He died for us and then was resurrected so that we can live again after we die. His sacrifice is called the Atonement (Alma 7:11–13; 34:8–9).

Through the Atonement, Jesus did His part to help us return to live with our Father in Heaven and be happy. Now we have to do our part. We need to take certain steps to show the Savior that we accept Him and will follow His commandments. These steps are called the first principles and ordinances of the gospel (2 Nephi 31:10–13).

Article of Faith 4 reads: "We believe that the first principles and ordinances of the Gospel are: first, Faith in the Lord Jesus Christ; second, Repentance; third, Baptism by immersion for the remission of sins; fourth, Laying on of hands for the gift of the Holy Ghost." Completing these steps and continuing to repent and have faith will lead us to make and keep temple covenants (D&C 124:36, 40). Then, if we endure to the end, we can live with our Heavenly Father and our families forever (2 Nephi 31:11–16; D&C 20:29).

The first principle of the gospel is faith in Jesus Christ. Faith is believing in something true that we cannot see (Joseph Smith Translation, Hebrews 11:1; Alma 32:21; Ether 12:4). Having faith in Jesus Christ means believing He is the Savior of the world and trusting in Him (Galatians 3:26).

The second principle of the gospel is repentance. As our faith in Christ grows, we will want to become more like Him. We will want to repent of our sins. When we repent, we feel sorry for what we have done and ask Heavenly Father and others for forgiveness (Alma 34:17). We do all we can to make things right and not repeat the sin.

After we have faith in Jesus Christ and repent of our sins, we are prepared for the first ordinance of the gospel— baptism. The word *ordinance* means a sacred act performed by priesthood authority. Baptism is a commandment given to us by our Father in Heaven. It is the gateway to the path that leads us back to Him (2 Nephi 31:17–18; D&C 20:37).

The ordinance of baptism is performed by worthy men who hold the priesthood. The priesthood is the authority to act in the name of God (Hebrews 5:4; D&C 13:1; Article of Faith 5).

Heavenly Father commands us to be baptized by immersion. *Immersion* means going completely under water. Baptism by immersion is a symbol of death and resurrection. It represents the end of our old life and the beginning of our new life as followers of Jesus Christ (Romans 6:3–6; D&C 20:73–74; 76:51–53).

Although Jesus was perfect, He was baptized to show His obedience to all of Heavenly Father's commandments. John the Baptist held the priesthood authority and baptized Jesus by immersion in the River Jordan (Matthew 3:13–17; 2 Nephi 31:4–11).

Heavenly Father has taught us that at eight years of age, children begin to be accountable for their actions. Babies and younger children do not need to be baptized because they cannot sin (D&C 29:46–47; 68:27).

Many people have died without being baptized. Because our Heavenly Father loves all His children, He offers them an opportunity to receive baptism. In sacred temples, members of The Church of Jesus Christ of Latter-day Saints can be baptized for family members and others who have died (D&C 128:16–17).

What are the promises we make at baptism?

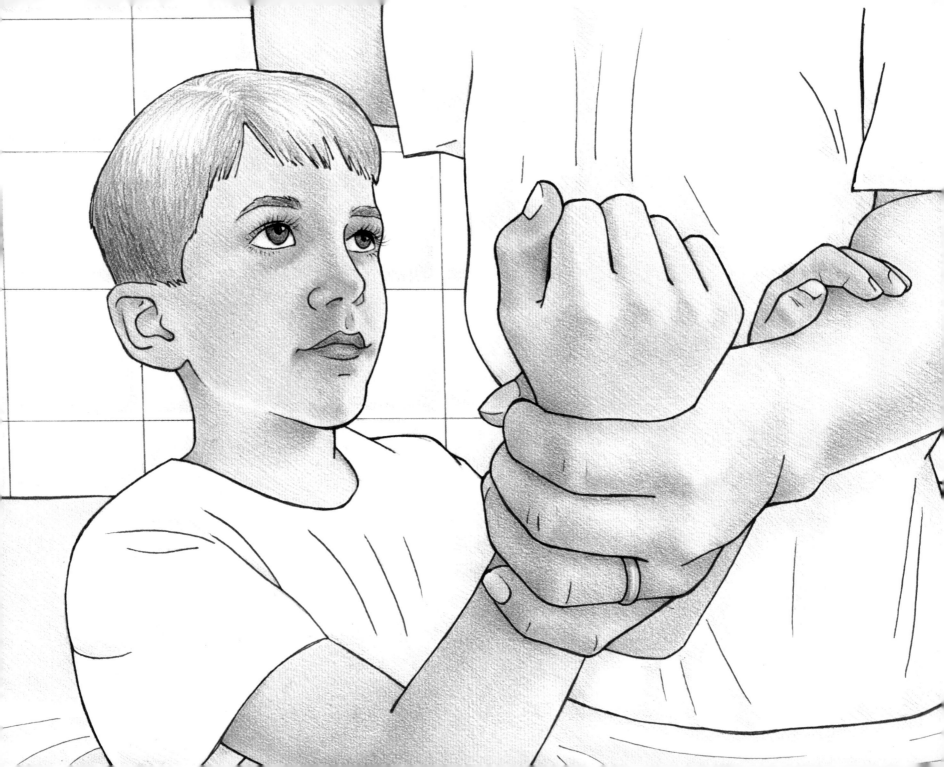

When I am baptized, I make a promise,
called a covenant, with my Heavenly Father.

Mosiah 5:5; Alma 7:15

I promise to—

Take upon myself the name of Jesus Christ.

Always remember Him.

Keep His commandments.

Serve Him and others.

Take upon myself the name of Jesus Christ.

This means I try to be like Jesus all the time because I represent Him.

Doctrine and Covenants 20:37

Always remember Him.

I always think of Jesus and remember His love for me. Then I will want to do what He wants me to do more than what I may want to do.

3 Nephi 18:11; Helaman 5:9–12

Keep His commandments.

I will obey His commandments "at all times and in all things, and in all places" (Mosiah 18:9).

Mosiah 18:8–10

Serve Him and others.

The best way to serve the Lord is to serve others: "When ye are in the service of your fellow beings ye are only in the service of your God" (Mosiah 2:17).

Matthew 25:40; Mosiah 18:8–10; Doctrine and Covenants 42:29

As I keep my baptismal promises,
Heavenly Father promises that—

The Holy Ghost will always be with me
when I do what is right.

My sins will be forgiven.

I can return to live with Him.

The Holy Ghost will always be with me
when I do what is right.

After I am baptized, I receive the gift of the Holy Ghost. He will always be with me when I do what is right.

2 Nephi 31:12; 2 Nephi 32:5; Moroni 10:5

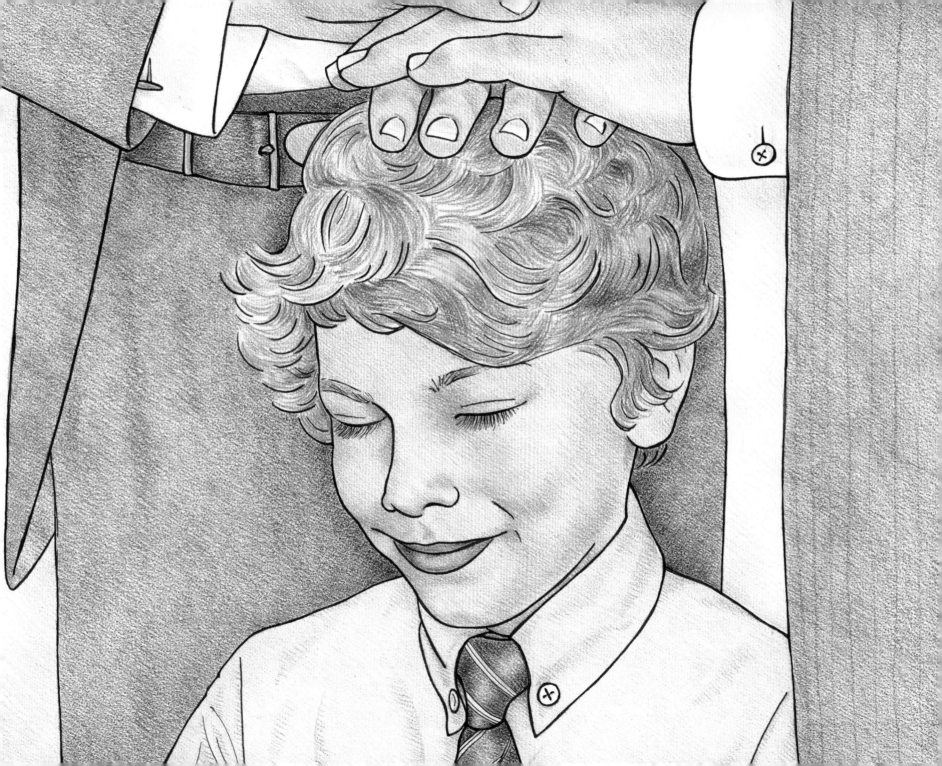

My sins will be forgiven.

After I have followed the steps of faith, repentance, and baptism, Heavenly Father will forgive me for all my sins because of Jesus' sacrifice for me in the Garden of Gethsemane and on the cross at Calvary. His sacrifice is called the Atonement.

2 Nephi 31:17; Moroni 8:25

I can return to live with Him.

Because of the Savior's Atonement, if I keep the promises I make at baptism and prepare to make and keep temple covenants, I can return to live with my Heavenly Father and my family forever.

2 Nephi 31:19–20; Alma 7:15–16;

Doctrine and Covenants 14:7; Moses 1:39

After I am baptized, Heavenly Father expects me to try my best to keep the promises I have made to Him so I can be happy.

2 Nephi 31:18–19; Alma 41:10

Our loving Father in Heaven knows
that even after I am baptized, I will make
mistakes and sin.

Ether 12:27; Doctrine and Covenants 62:1

As I take the sacrament each Sunday, I remember the promises I made to Heavenly Father when I was baptized. Because of the Savior's Atonement, if I repent, I can become as pure as I was the day I was baptized.

Doctrine and Covenants 20:77, 79

Through baptism and confirmation by
priesthood authority, I also become a member of
The Church of Jesus Christ of Latter-day Saints.

Mosiah 18:17; Doctrine and Covenants 20:37

Through the ordinance of baptism, I am born again into a new life of righteousness. Just as a baby begins a new life when he or she is born into mortality, so I begin a new life after I am baptized. By keeping my baptismal covenants, I can become more like the Savior, Jesus Christ.

John 3:5; Romans 6:4; Mosiah 27:25–26; Alma 7:14; Moses 6:59

I am thankful for the
promises I make
at baptism.

I promise to—

Take upon myself the name of Jesus Christ.

Always remember Him.

Keep His commandments.

Serve Him and others.

Heavenly Father promises that—

*The Holy Ghost will always be with me
when I do what is right.*

My sins will be forgiven.

I can return to live with Him.

ABOUT THE AUTHOR

Michele Leigh Carnesecca served a mission in Mexico and received an RN degree from Utah State and Weber State Universities. She works for Intermountain Health Care and has taught classes around the country on women's health issues. She is the author of *How Does the Holy Ghost Make Me Feel?* the companion volume to *What Are the Promises I Make at Baptism?* She lives in Cedar Hills, Utah, with her husband, Chad, and their four children.

ABOUT THE ILLUSTRATOR

Carol Shelley Xanthos earned her BFA in illustration from Brigham Young University. She is the illustrator of *How Does the Holy Ghost Make Me Feel?* the companion volume to *What Are the Promises I Make at Baptism?* She lives with her husband, George, and their five sons in Beaverton, Oregon.